4332

D1268643

Fairway Elementary
480 Old Fairway Drive
Wildwood, MO 63040
636-458-7300

WITHDRAWN

Animal Opposites

Loud
and
Quiet

An Animal Opposites Book

by Lisa Bullard

consulting editor: Gail Saunders-Smith, PhD
content consultant: Zoological Society of San Diego

Capstone press

Mankato, Minnesota

Some animals make sounds as loud
as thunder. Others are so quiet
they hardly make any noise at all.
Let's learn about loud and quiet
by looking at animals around the world.

Loud

Whales sing loudly as they swim in the ocean. Their whistles and cries can be heard hundreds of miles away.

Quiet

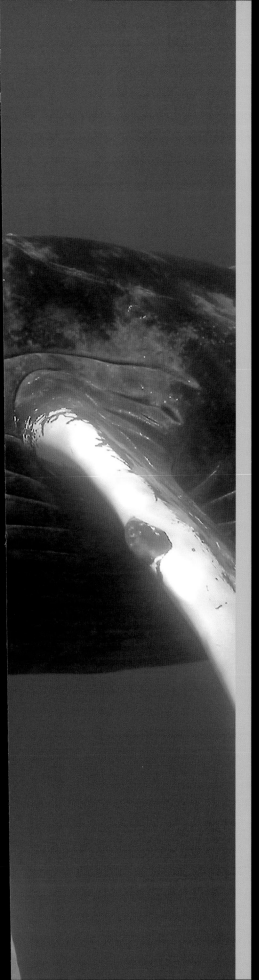

Bats seem to fly quietly
through the night.
But they make noises
that people can't hear.

Many whales and bats
use sounds to find
food. They listen for
sounds to echo off the
fish or bugs they eat.

Loud

Howler monkeys swing
through rain forest trees.
They howl loudly
to tell other monkeys,
"Stay away from me!"

Quiet

Knifefish swim quietly
through rain forest rivers.

Loud

Spring peepers sing to each other.
Their loud peeps are a sign
that spring has begun.

Quiet fireflies are also called lightning bugs. But don't expect them to make any thunder.

Fireflies blink on and off to send messages to other fireflies.

Loud

Sea lions crawl up on shore to lie in the sun. They bark loudly to claim their spot on the beach.

Squids swim quietly through
dark ocean waters.

When some squids
are angry or afraid,
they change colors.

Loud

Gray wolves howl loudly
to call out to members
of their pack.

Quiet

Caribou roam across the plains.
They stay quiet, so hungry
wolves won't hear them.

Loud

Male cicadas are the world's loudest insects. Some cicadas are as loud as lawn mowers.

Butterflies are quiet.
They flash bright colors
as they fly across the sky.

Loud

Most owls hunt at night
and sleep during the day.
But barred owls hoot loudly
both night and day.

Quiet

Being quiet as a mouse
isn't always quiet enough.
This mouse might become
an owl snack.

Loud

Rattlesnakes loudly shake their tails to warn other animals to stay away.

Each time a rattlesnake sheds its skin, a new section of rattle appears.

Most other snakes quietly slither away from danger.

Loud

Woodpeckers hammer loudly on trees with their beaks.

Woodpeckers peck at trees to find food. They're looking for ants and other bugs.

Ants are quiet insects that crawl everywhere.

Loud

Parrots squawk loudly
to say hello to each other.

Quiet

Wood storks quietly
wade in water.
They can't sing
or squawk like
other birds.

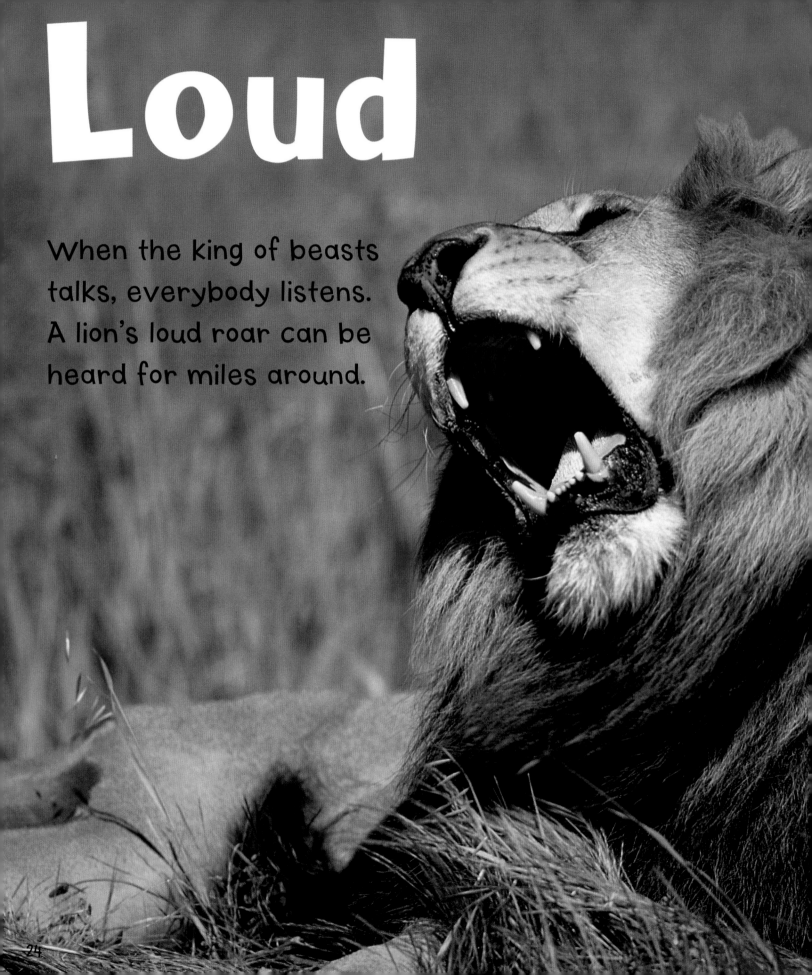

Loud

When the king of beasts talks, everybody listens. A lion's loud roar can be heard for miles around.

Chameleons quietly
creep through trees.
They sneak up on
the bugs they eat.

Some animals squawk loudly
to say hello. Others howl and roar.
Some animals stay safe by keeping
quiet. Others sneak through forests
as they hunt for food.

What kinds of loud and quiet animals live near you?

Did You Know?

Many animals use sounds to communicate. But animals have other ways to send messages, such as body movements and color changes. Dogs wag their tails to show they're excited. Chameleons tell other animals they're angry by changing color.

Some animals make sounds that are too low for people to hear. These animals include elephants, giraffes, hippos, whales, tigers, and chameleons.

Scientists compare the loudness of different sounds using measurements called decibels. People talk at 60 to 70 decibels. Jet engines can be as loud as 140 decibels. The loudest animals, blue whales, have made sounds that measured 188 decibels.

Monarch butterflies don't make sounds to communicate. But their orange-and-black markings send a message. The colors tell other animals that monarch butterflies taste bad.

People who are deaf use a form of communication called sign language. Sign language is a way of talking with hand signals. Scientists are now studying gorillas and chimpanzees to learn whether some animals can communicate by using sign language.

Glossary

communicate (kuh-myoo-nih-KAYT)—to share facts, ideas, or feelings

decibel (DESS-uh-bel)—a unit for measuring how loud or quiet sounds are

echo (EK-oh)—sound waves that bounce off objects and return to the listener

insect (IN-sekt)—a small animal with a hard outer shell, six legs, three body sections, and two antennas; most insects have wings.

message (MESS-ij)—facts, ideas, or feelings sent to someone or something

rattle (RAT-uhl)—the end part of a rattlesnake's tail that produces a rattling sound

Read More

Dahl, Michael. *Do Bears Buzz?: A Book about Animal Sounds.* Animals all Around. Minneapolis: Picture Window Books, 2003.

Deegan, Kim. *My First Book of Opposites.* New York: Bloomsbury Children's Books, 2002.

Jenkins, Steve. *Slap, Squeak, & Scatter: How Animals Communicate.* Boston: Houghton Mifflin, 2001.

Internet Sites

FactHound offers a safe, fun way to find Internet sites related to this book. All of the sites on FactHound have been researched by our staff.

Here's how:

1. Visit *www.facthound.com*

2. Type in this special code **0736842764** for age-appropriate sites. Or enter a search word related to this book for a more general search.

3. Click on the **Fetch It** button.

FactHound will fetch the best sites for you!

Index

A+ Books are published by Capstone Press,
151 Good Counsel Drive, P.O. Box 669, Mankato, Minnesota 56002.
www.capstonepress.com

Copyright © 2006 Capstone Press. All rights reserved.
No part of this publication may be reproduced in whole or in part, or stored in a retrieval system, transmitted in any form or by any means, electronic, mechanical, photocopying, recording, or otherwise, without written permission of the publisher. For information regarding permission, write Capstone Press, 151 Good Counsel Drive,
P.O. Box 669, Dept. R, Mankato, Minnesota 56002.
Printed in the United States of America

1 2 3 4 5 6 10 09 08 07 06 05

Library of Congress Cataloging-in-Publication Data
Bullard, Lisa.
Loud and quiet: an animal opposites book / by Lisa Bullard.
p. cm.—(A+ books. Animal opposites.)
Includes bibliographical references and index.
ISBN 0-7368-4276-4 (hardcover)
1. Animal sounds—Juvenile literature. I. Title. II. Series.
QL765.B83 2006
591.59'4—dc22   2004027951

Summary: Brief text introduces the concepts of loud and quiet, comparing some of the world's loudest animals with animals that are quiet.

Credits
Blake A. Hoena, editor; Kia Adams, designer; Kelly Garvin, photo researcher;
Scott Thoms, photo editor

Photo Credits
Bruce Coleman Inc./Dale R. Thompson, 21; Bruce Coleman Inc./Don Mammoser, 17; Bruce Coleman Inc./Gail M. Shumway, 16; Bruce Coleman Inc./Hans Reinhard, 7; Bruce Coleman Inc./Joe McDonald, 20; Bruce Coleman Inc./John Shaw, 13; Bruce Coleman Inc./S. C. Bisserot, 5; Corbis/Aron Frankental/Gallo Images, 14; Corel, 1 (frog), 3 (frog), 26 (cicada), 27 (rattlesnake), 27 (squid); Creatas, 2 (caribou); Digital Vision Ltd./Gerry Ellis, 2 (wolf); Digital Vision Ltd./Gerry Ellis & Michael Durham, 1 (chameleon), 26 (chameleon); Dwight Kuhn, 8, 9; Getty Images Inc./Joseph Van Os, 24; Image Ideas, 1 (lion), 3 (lion); J.H. Pete Carmichael, 25; Minden Pictures/Claus Meyer, 22; Minden Pictures/Jim Brandenburg, 15; Peter Arnold/Martin Harvey, cover (lion); Photodisc, 3 (butterfly), 29; Photodisc/G.K. & Vikki Hart, 27 (parrot); Root Resources/Mary Root, cover (malachite); Seapics.com/James D. Watt, 4; Seapics.com/Jeff Jaskolski, 11; Tom & Pat Leeson, 6; Tom Stack & Associates, Inc./Barbara Gerlach, 10 ; Tom Stack & Associates, Inc./Joe McDonald, 18; Tom Stack & Associates, Inc./Tom & Therisa Stack, 23; Visuals Unlimited/David Campbell, 19; Visuals Unlimited/Tom Walker, 12

Note to Parents, Teachers, and Librarians

This Animal Opposites book uses full-color photographs and a nonfiction format to introduce children to the concepts of loud and quiet. *Loud and Quiet* is designed to be read aloud to a pre-reader or to be read independently by an early reader. Photographs help listeners and early readers understand the text and concepts discussed. The book encourages further learning by including the following sections: Did You Know?, Glossary, Read More, Internet Sites, and Index. Early readers may need assistance using these features.

Fairway Elementary
480 Old Fairway Drive
Wildwood, MO 63040
636-458-7300

WITHDRAWN